FROGS
AND OTHER
SOUL FRIENDS

*Reflections
from the Forest*

NANCY R. CANNON

Frogs and Other Soul Friends: Reflections from the Forest

ISBN: 978-1478234555

First Edition: November 2012

Photography by Nancy R. Cannon.

Printed in the United States of America.

This book is dedicated to our beloved granddaughter, Julia Lily,
with every hope and prayer that her grandchildren will still
be able to experience these wilderness wonders.

CONTENTS

PREFACE

The stories that unfold in the following pages took place in our woods in rural Michigan. With its white pine forest, wild berry thickets, old growth hemlocks, small pond, and winding creek that flows year-round, this land provides for an extraordinary diversity of wildlife encounters.

Despite the fact that I refer to many of the creatures in these stories as "friends," I don't want to confuse the reader. They are in no way domesticated. All of the creatures are wild, and they come and go freely. I use the word "friend" because it most adequately conveys the deep and personal connection I feel with so many of them.

When referring to wild creatures, indigenous people have used the word "relatives" or "relations." Saint Francis of Assisi addressed creatures as his "brothers and sisters." I appreciate all these terms because they convey such an important and often overlooked reality: all the creatures found in the wild are part of our extended family. We share the same land as one community. The earth is not ours, nor is it theirs. It belongs to all of us - together!

Other wild beings are truly our neighbors. They deserve to be treated with the same care and respect one would hopefully show a human neighbor. Aren't they actually better neighbors than most? They don't take more than their share, they aren't too noisy, they don't leave trash, and most importantly, they do not destroy our mutual home, this earth.

It is my prayer, and the deepest longing of my heart that we, the human ones, might one day be worthy to be called *their* friends and *their* good neighbors as well.

I never consciously set out to write a book, but so many people encouraged me to share these reflections and photos with a larger audience. I am so grateful they did. I want to acknowledge all of you:

My cherished friends, both of my women's groups, and my spiritual direction peer group. Thank you so much for reading my writings and for responding with so much enthusiasm. You helped me believe I have something valuable to share.

Special thanks to my family members, Daniel, Chrissy, Jim, and Jane, for your love and support, and for all the ways you honor the earth.

There are three other family members who have made such significant contributions to this book that I must mention them individually.

First, I want to thank my dearest sister, Barbara, for her devotion in faithfully deliberating with me over every aspect of this book. As my editor, no comma or colon escaped her scrutiny. If any errors remain, surely they were added after she finished editing.

I especially want to acknowledge our youngest son, Justin, who has been so generous with his time and talents. This book would not have been born without his gentle prodding, encouragement, and technical expertise. His publishing experience has led the way for me to share my heart in this book, and for that I am forever grateful.

Last of all, I want to thank my beloved husband, Richard, who has been supportive of this endeavor in more ways than I can convey. I feel so fortunate to be married to my soul mate and nature companion who not only attentively read, but also experienced so many of these stories with me. He is always ready to share my joy when I say, "Richard, hurry, come see."

"The universe is composed of subjects to be communed with, not objects to be exploited. Everything has its own voice. Thunder and lightning and stars and planets, flowers, birds, animals, trees – all these have voices, and they constitute a community of existence that is profoundly related."

—Thomas Berry

FROGS
AND OTHER
SOUL FRIENDS

*Reflections
from the Forest*

FROG CONTEMPLATIVES

Watching two green frogs in our pond,
I grow weary with empathy.
Spring is beginning
And they are hungry.
All day long they sit in the same spot
Waiting and waiting some more.
Occasionally a bug flies near enough
To be trapped by their long silky tongues.
They chew, swallow, and return to
Their job of being as still as
The rock on which they rest.

I would love to climb inside their thoughts.
Do they have thoughts?
Are they bored?
Are they doing frog meditation?
Are they enjoying the moment?
Are they frustrated that gratification is so infrequent?
Are they at peace?

In order to eat they have to remain
Completely passive.
And yet they must remain
Attentive and alert to
That one moment when they must be
Precisely active.
In that second they must gather
All their energy and focus.
They must be totally
Accurate in their timing and in their aim
If they are to seize the bug.

Could a martial arts expert be more disciplined
Than this frog that knows when to be still
And when to act?
Could a deep contemplative be more at peace
In the silence and stillness?
Could a saint be more confident
That daily bread will be provided
Without the need to strive?
Could I have a better role model as I seek to learn?
Only when rooted in deep silence and stillness
Will I find the composure to act
With wisdom and discernment.

SNAKE FOOD

The frogs in our pond are a daily sight now that spring's warmth has arrived. Each morning I rise and greet them for the Daily Frog Count. We had three guests in our little pond this winter. I treated them well with a "hot tub" among other amenities. Were it not electrically heated, this shallow artificial pond would freeze over completely and the green frogs would suffocate. So, for the delight of having frog friends near, I figure the added cost is a meager sacrifice.

Having waited five months for the taste of fresh live bugs, these frogs show amazing patience. For hours they sit still, barely moving at all, hoping that a bug will fly into their expansive view. I rarely see them catch anything at all, but this day was different. I stood beside the pond with the usual awe and delight when suddenly the biggest green frog, obscured by the ground cover, leapt to his side with tongue extended – chewing with his big jaws – smirking! Actually it happened so fast that all I remember is seeing his huge pink tongue. Surprisingly, I felt like cheering for the frog. His patience had been rewarded.

As if that were not enough of a treat, frog #2 surprised me as well. These frogs rarely make a sound. I'm not sure why, but when I came near, he began croaking at me. Each time he croaked, I croaked back at him. This went on for a minute or two. I found myself saying the silliest things, "Well, hello! I'm glad to see you too. How have *you* been?" Each ridiculous question received a long croak in reply. For all I know, he was telling me to leave so I wouldn't scare away the bugs, but I don't think so. I think he was saying, "Hi, it's me, Freddie, the one you named three years ago. I'm still here. That's my son over there. I still like living here." I don't speak "frog" as well as Freddie, of course, but I do know we were interacting. For now, that is enough. But my story doesn't end there. That was all this morning. It is evening now and my frog count of three is coming up one short. I can't find frog #3. I know all the places to look: the little rocky hill covered with sedum, the potted plants still in the pond, over by the heater, and around the rim of the pond. It is nowhere to be found. My mind leaps, as it always does, to the thought of the resident garter snakes. I haven't seen them yet this year, but they could easily be lurking out of view.

Why do I rejoice with the frog when he catches a bug, but ache inside at the thought of one of my friends being dinner for a hungry snake? The snakes are wondrous creatures as well and certainly deserve a meal, but I have been known to grab them by the tail and pull them away as they approach my frog friends. I can't help it! I am a hopelessly loyal friend, and the frogs have captured my heart.

I know it is the way of the Grand Design that one should eat or be eaten. I realize I must make peace with that if I am truly to accept Nature in all its glory. But, how can I detach and distance myself from such a personal love for each frog? I would have to step back and love them all equally as One – the frogs, the snakes, the trees, the All.

If I can't detach from a frog, how will I ever detach from my family, my friends, and from my own life when it is time for me to go? How will I ever learn how to love this life passionately and let it go – all in one big continuous dance – loving, letting go, loving more, and letting go again? I don't know, but it appears that I've been given the opportunity to practice with these fragile little green frogs who are so at home in the stillness and serenity of the moment.

FROG CHORUS

It is just getting dark as I grab my groceries and prepare to walk across the massive parking lot that surrounds the grocery store. As I drive away, even with the windows closed, a mysterious sound causes me to make a u-turn and travel to the farthest and most remote part of the parking lot.

In the distance the setting sun is spreading a wash of yellow, orange, pink, and purple across the sky, the perfect canvas for the intricate tree branches forming pen and ink silhouettes. To my left, barely hidden behind the delicate barrier of tall graceful grasses, I discover hundreds of chorus frogs making their loud melody, doing their best to live up to their name. I'm told they are competing, trying to attract a mate with the most impressive song. Were I one of the frogs, it would be terribly hard to choose as so many melodies lure me from one to the next. Their singing may be in competition, but I also hear harmony and a few solo artists performing their Frog Oratorio.

I'm not so sure that they are singing their choruses to lure a mate. Personally, I think they are rejoicing that the lights are dimming, that people are leaving, and that car engines are retreating. The dimness of light spreads a blanket of calm on this concrete chaos. Even the distant sound of a motorcycle is dulled by the jubilant songs of the Frog Chorus. For a few moments, serenity has conquered the insanity. For a few moments the frog choruses have transported me, and I am no longer in a parking lot in Michigan.

I am somewhere long ago and far away. I am in a swampy land of open spaces, clean crisp air, and endless expanses of wilderness. I am carried away with this chorus, swelling with gratitude. I am an observer no longer but rather a participant. I am part of their sacred ritual, an annual rite of music making en masse. Or perhaps I should say frog "mass" music! I am in a world of sweet smells, gentle skies, and restful rhythms.

As I reluctantly return to Michigan, to the parking lot, to now, a fearful thought invades my joy. Will this sacred space one day be forfeited for a larger parking lot? All I know is that like a flower, persistently growing through a concrete sidewalk, this Frog Chorus is being conducted by One who will not be silenced.

DRAGONFLY DRAMA

Walking through our woods, I notice a dragonfly is perched on my arm. My initial delight is short-lived. Something is wrong. Its body is attached to the left wing and the two right wings are also stuck together. I look more closely and notice tiny spider web threads causing this poor dragonfly to be crippled. It escaped death, but now it is terribly stuck. It readily climbs onto the stick I offer so that I can get a better look.

"Please don't leave," I say to the dragonfly hoping it will somehow get the message that I want to help. Another part of me has the strange feeling that it has, in fact, come to me for that very purpose. So I walk to the door and holler to my husband who is indoors. "Richard, quick, I need my glasses and some scissors, hurry!" I yell, neglecting to even say please. He arrives in time for me to cut the strand that frees the tail from the wings. This is the easy part I realize. It has now been five minutes at least, and the dragonfly is still staying with me. Then it seems to be testing out the new freedom only to awkwardly land on the grass again. There it struggles and my heart sinks.

So I offer it the stick again hoping it will crawl on and let me look more closely. It does. Each time it falls, it crawls back onto my stick and then eventually onto my fingers. I sense we are both determined to overcome this struggle. As it rests on my fingers, I see that the left wings are fine, but the right wings are so glued together that it will be a major challenge to free them. This will require my fine cuticle scissors, so once again I holler, "Richa-a-a-rd, hurry." Being the avid nature lover he is, he is quickly at my side with everything we need for the next steps.

This dragonfly is hanging around an amazingly long time. Each time a web strand is cut, it seems to flinch and wiggle as if struggling, but it doesn't jump away. It is as if it understands. It has been at least ten minutes or more by now. My deepest intuition is that the dragonfly is willing for me to do whatever it takes to release the wings.

It waits as I try to gently slide the scissors between the two wings. It won't work. I am afraid I will have to cut, but I don't want to cut the fragile wings. I'm scared but determined. So I take the spray bottle of water and gently mist this delicate creature. I'm not sure why, but it feels like a good thing to do. I see its tiny legs as they wipe across its huge eyes. I also see a funny thing that looks like a mouth. Then it looks in my direction as if looking at me. Does it see me? Does it feel me? Does it truly understand that I am doing my best to help? To me it feels like the answer is "yes." To my surprise, my husband (who is more likely to say "maybe") totally agrees with me that the dragonfly has come for help. It seems to trust me. I am awed by such a thought. But I am also terribly afraid to fail or to hurt such an amazing creature.

Finally it perches on my fingertips and I have the sense that now is the time. Go for it. Release the other two wings no matter what it takes. I get the sense that the dragonfly is in accord. It has been at least fifteen minutes. It is time to finish the job. So sliding the tips of the cuticle scissors between the two wings, I allow them to ever so slightly clip. Then, to my total surprise, mid cut, the dragonfly ascends straight up for the first time. It is flying high out of view. I am elated as I walk into the house once again yelling for Richard. But this time I am yelling with glee.

"Richard, Richard, it worked! The dragonfly flew away! I can't believe it! I think it really did come for help. It trusted me and we did it! It's a miracle!"

HIDDEN PICTURES

So often our woods lures me into the most delightful game of "hidden pictures." Our small house is surrounded by eight acres of land so I can look out any window and see forest within twenty or thirty feet. Often the game of "hidden pictures" lasts no more than a few moments, but today the game went on for at least half an hour.

It began with the sight of two ears of a deer that I had mistaken for tree branches. As the deer's form finally unveiled itself to me, I became glued to the window. It was a young deer that had chosen the best view on our property. It was resting on the hill among the hemlocks that overlook the winding creek. It wasn't sleeping but rather resting while scanning the view. As I watched, I could almost feel myself alongside the deer, as I know that spot so well. I could feel the crispness of the air tempered by the sun's warmth. I could smell the scent of pine and hear the music of the creek now flowing with an abundance of thawed snow. I could feel the serenity of being fully present with the deer – no duties to fulfill, no meetings to attend, and no reason to hurry.

Then another deer sauntered into the vista. Had it been there all along? I don't know, but it was as if I put on the glasses at a 3-D movie and became awake to the idea that more deer were in the woods. Their greatest defense is their ability to move discreetly and blend into the environment. Their skinny legs precisely mirror the size of the young new saplings and their brown shades of fur blend perfectly with the tree bark. It is easy to stare right at them without seeing them. But I am getting pretty good at this game, and gradually I was able to see all seven deer spaced throughout the hemlock hill. Having spent a luxurious amount of time observing their enviable lifestyle, I decided I needed to return to my own. I left them to enjoy their late morning rest.

It was time to attend to my chores. My first job was to put the big bag of birdseed into the metal garbage can on the porch. In the process of doing so, I managed to drop the lid and send it crashing into the can. It sent the harshest, clanging sound into the peaceful forest. In fact it was such a loud piercing sound, it resembled that of a gunshot. Knowing I had surely ruined the deer's rest, I sheepishly returned to the window for another view. Yes, I had ruined the moment. Now all the deer were on their feet, standing at attention, and looking in my direction. They were clearly alarmed and motionless in self-defense.

In that moment, I realized there are very few harsh sounds in nature. It is only we humans who have brought sound pollution. Yes, other creatures can be noisy, but it is the human sounds that are the most disturbing and harsh: the truck engines on the highway, the sirens, the alarms, the mowers, and worst of all, the gunshots. I felt ashamed of all these intrusions into the other creatures' peaceful lives. I can be very sensitive about noise when other people are resting. Why didn't I show more concern for the resting deer?

I am reminded of indigenous people who truly understand that other creatures are our brothers and our sisters. The deer are our relatives. We share the same land with them. This land is truly theirs as well as ours. We are part of one community. I must be more mindful of their lifestyle as I live out my own.

ANNUAL RETURN

We have the most extraordinary guests who visit us each year. They appear in May and fill our trees with brilliant colorful accents. I have always delighted at the return of the orioles, the rose-breasted grosbeaks and the indigo buntings as well as the wrens and the hummers. But just recently, I have begun to fathom the incredible effort they must make to arrive among us. I find their journey nothing short of heroic. They make their pilgrimage on pure stamina and determination. Yes, it is also instinct, but many do not survive the ordeal.

They spend their winters in Central and South America and must travel over one thousand miles to arrive here in Michigan. They must pass through storms and fly despite exhaustion. So when they arrive, I am so thrilled I want to sound the trumpets. Like athletes who survive the adversity of the long distance run, these birds deserve a grand celebration. As of yet, all I have known to do is keep the feeders full and fresh water available. Perhaps keeping their habitat clean and untouched is the best way I can honor these courageous travelers.

The rose-breasted grosbeaks were the first to arrive this year and they have settled into their domestic duties as a team. Rose-breasted grosbeaks mate for life and both of them tend their young. At the next celebration, they will have to get special recognition for their equal partnership. I have been watching for the indigo bunting that lights up our trees like a radiant jewel. I had begun to doubt his arrival as it is almost June now, but today he arrived and is flaunting his brilliant plumage. No other bird can compare to his blue iridescence.

The wrens have arrived as well and are filling the woods with the most glorious music. It seems there has been an equitable distribution of gifts. The birds that have the most beautiful songs are often those with the least colorful feathers. They usually dress in various shades of brown. There is no better song to awaken to than that of a wren. I am filled with such deep gratitude when these birds select our piece of land for their visit.

What amazing divine plan guides them here each year? How grand that such a plan could exist, that both hemispheres would be graced by the presence of such extraordinary creatures. It could easily have been different. We could have been left with only the winter birds throughout the year. But, as it is, diversity and interdependence are part of the design. These birds were doing cross-cultural visitation long before we learned how to fly. Will we ever learn from these seasoned travelers – to leave no damage, to eat only what we need, to spread beauty by our presence, to trust our needs will be met, and to be friends with others on the opposite side of the world?

BIRTHING

There is a robin nesting in our garage only eight feet from our parked car. Upon returning last night, she almost dive-bombed me with her sharp beak. She is already resting on the nest so we certainly can't move her. And of course, there is always the lingering question. Whose garage is it anyway? Yes, we lived here first, but she doesn't know that. She doesn't know about ownership of huge spaces or about the imaginary lines we create in the woods.

I'm sure she considered the fact that no other bird was nesting nearby. I'm sure she fulfilled all the creature protocols. How can we expect her to know the human rules? To her, we are the invaders who obviously show no respect when nearing the maternity ward. How will we co-exist during this tenuous time? I know how she feels. It is hard enough to birth babies much less fearing for your safety at the same time. We will have to reassure her somehow as we learn to share the garage.

Now it is a week later. The babies are born and the mother seems more at ease. We can go in and out quietly without causing her to panic. I was surprised to discover the babies had hatched as she is still faithfully sitting on them. She leaves from time to time and returns with something in her beak, but then she sits on them again. She must position herself so carefully so as not to smother them. It has been cool lately so perhaps they are grateful for the warmth of her feathers.

My life has been altered a little due to her presence. I must do some of my artwork outdoors at times to give her adequate space. But I don't mind. I've given birth to two babies and breastfed each for a long time. Those tasks are challenging enough without the added stress of frightening neighbors. The mother in me feels an affinity with the mother in her and I would gladly go way out of my way to lighten her load. I understand her devotion and honor it.

There's a part of me that dreads the process of these babies growing and eventually flying. I know it is common for some to fall from the nest and die. I know this personally as I have strong early memories of watching my mother feed a baby bird with an eyedropper. I also remember her weeping, as it did not survive. I, too, spent many days nursing a baby chickadee – feeding it by hand many times a day and eventually releasing it. I was fortunate as my experience had a happy ending. But it required intense devotion over many days.

It is evening now and I made the most wonderful discovery. The mother robin is not alone in the task of feeding the babies. It appears she has an equally devoted husband who shares the duties. I am so genuinely happy for her. Every female who labors over birth deserves the unfailing support of a partner who is equally devoted, not only to the babies, but to her as well. I assume it is their father. I am so happy for him too. How sad it would be for him to miss out on nurturing his offspring.

It is now a week later and this is the big day! Passing through the garage, I see several huge "baby" robins tottering on the edge of their nest. I know this will be their launching day. Knowing they need room to spread their wings, I watch from the distance with binoculars. How jubilant I am to see them leave, to look into their empty nest. But the jubilation is short-lived. One lone bird is hovering in the corner of the garage. Its only hope is for me to leave so that it can hop out into the daylight and fly away.

Hours later, I am returning with baby food in hand in case I have to deal with an orphan. As I look around the garage I breathe a sigh of relief. It is nowhere to be found. But then I notice. It is perched on a bucket in the driveway. My heart sinks! It is clearly confused and waiting. Pondering what to do, I decide to approach the bird to see if it is afraid of me. At my final approach it soars away into the treetops where another robin is waiting. I am elated. Somehow nature managed to unfold without my assistance. How humbling, and what a relief!

MAGICAL MOMENTS

I awoke to a seemingly ordinary day, but by its end I had been touched by nothing short of magic, not once, but twice! I don't think one can go looking for magical moments, as they seem to come as gift, but I find they often arrive on the heels of curiosity. Curiosity is part of our human inheritance, but too often it gets left behind with childhood. On this day, curiosity served me well.

I was sitting outside where I often work on writing or art. This time it was writing. The day was as perfect as early summer can get in Michigan: cool, breezy, sunny, and bright. It was the slight commotion in our pine forest that made me curious and alerted me to visitors. As I focused my gaze, a mother deer and two fawns came into view. The fawns were so tiny and speckled; I almost thought they were brand-new. But when I noticed they moved so easily, I realized they must have been at least a few days old. Suddenly, a show started. One of the little ones began to run and leap and bound across the carpet of soft pine needles. It was running in huge circles past the mother and the other baby, leaping over logs and charging as if being pursued. But there was no predator, only a baby deer discovering the joy of running for the pure bliss of running. Was it running for the first time? Was it just discovering what legs can do? Had I not looked carefully, I might have assumed I was witnessing perky little puppies at play. The scene only lasted a couple minutes, but it stayed with me all day. Watching baby deer playing is enough to fill me with joy, but later my cup was filled to overflowing.

Evening came and it wasn't dark yet, but would be soon. Once again I heard sounds that seemed abnormal. There was a huge bird alarm going on, but it seemed different than the frequent fuss made by crows or jays. Led by curiosity, I slowly descended the trail that leads to the creek. The forest is a bit mysterious at that time of night so shadows can easily be mistaken for creatures. Knowing that, I looked very carefully at the bird that swooped down on the branch only eight feet above me. It looked like a very little owl, but I know how everything can look like a little owl when you glance casually at dusk. It was the robin that arrived on a nearby branch that gave me a clue. The robin was upset and clearly trying to scare the other bird away. But it did not go away. Instead it kept flitting from branch to branch, remaining amazingly close to me.

The whole event unfolded with so much mystery and enchantment. All I remember is turning in circles, straining to catch all the sights and sounds that encircled me so near. I was under the hemlock tree that grows right next to the creek. Above me, no more than nine feet away, I could hear the softest sounds. It was as if someone was breathing with a raspy breath or like someone was softly snoring with a wheezing trill in the snore. I saw the bird more and more clearly, but the sound seemed to keep moving and shifting location. Bird ventriloquism? Then it dawned on me that there was more than one bird. The images all came into focus gradually. The big one had a fat head, two upright ears, and was no more than eight inches tall. I knew I was seeing the mother screech owl and the other two were her fluffy little fledglings making their "feed me" call. No wonder she came so close to me. Unknowingly I had come near her babies. Despite the aggressive squawking of the robin, the mother remained attentive to her little ones that sang their soft "snoring" chorus. It was almost as if they were purring.

There is something about standing in the middle of a hemlock forest at dusk, watching and listening to nearby eastern screech owls, that left me feeling I was in the realm of pure Mystery. The child in me was so swept away that I almost expected the owl to land on my shoulder and offer a word of wisdom. Of course it didn't, but I am still left with the exquisite sense that it was as curious about me as I was about it. It seemed we were both watching and even staring at each other for long moments. And the connection went beyond staring. There was something huge going forth from my heart. Love might be too strong a word, but I did feel the most intense awe and respect for the creature and the deepest gratitude for our encounter. Could it possibly have felt my heart response? Of course I will never know, but I hope so. I hope it could feel how grateful I am that such a creature exists and has blessed our world with its presence.

LADYBUGS

Each year the ladybugs crawl into the crevices of our home, finding refuge from the harshness of winter in Michigan. Usually they hide from my awareness, but when the wood-burning stove causes our home to get toasty warm, they make their appearance. Drawn to the sunlight, they speckle the windows with their presence, seeking an exit into the seemingly sunny warmth nearby.

But I know better. Were they to get outside, they would be unprepared for the bitter cold and would probably die quickly. So I appease them a bit and sprinkle drops of water on the windows. Each of them finds their own water drop and begins consuming relatively huge amounts of water, sometimes equaling their size.

On those rare Michigan spring days that are balmy and warm, I begin my ladybug mission. I catch each bug in a little box and take it outside where it can fly toward the sun. Most of the ladybugs depart immediately with seeming delight, but some of them seem to prefer staying in the box. They aren't ready so I bring them back in the house, but some day they will have to leave when given the chance or else leave with a little force on my part.

About the time that I am transporting them to the new world in the dark little box, the analogy to my own life becomes glaringly apparent. I am sure the ladybugs experience my intervention as frightening. Trapped in the small box, they must assume that an enemy has captured them. And then amidst their turmoil, they are delivered into the very state for which they have yearned.

Sometimes the Hand of Life scoops me up into a dark box and I scream and kick and struggle. I can't see the Gentle Hands, so I assume my life is in the grip of a darkness that is consuming me. I cannot see those hands slipping me into the box and holding me securely as I am carried to a new place of warmth and light. In fact there are times when, like the ladybug, I remain in the box even when the lid has been removed. I prefer the confines of a predictable familiar space to the uncertainty of the unknown.

When I take off the lid I often say, "fly free little lady bug" and urge them onward. When they are reluctant, I gently blow on them a little to give them a nudge. Even then, some won't leave. I see myself in their reluctance. But I want to stop struggling when the box surrounds me. I want to stop fearing when the lid causes darkness. I want to trust that I am being carried by Gentle Hands and I want to fly free when the lid is removed. And when the time comes that I am facing my last moments, I want to trust the One who will "blow on me a little" and send me on my way unencumbered, free to soar with no more boxes and no more lids.

CHIPMUNKS

As I stepped out on the porch, I unexpectedly caught the gaze of a little chipmunk who was hunting stray birdseed. His eyes seemed to say, "Maybe if I'm real still she won't notice me." But I couldn't help notice the white-streaked creature with the shiny red fur and big black bright eyes that was maybe six feet away. My instinct was to soothe him, so I spoke in that high-pitched voice that mothers reserve for fussy babies. The sound startled him, but clearly he was conflicted or perhaps curious about such a big creature with such a little squeaky voice. I quickly sat on the steps and made myself as little and non-threatening as possible. Surprisingly he didn't flee, and as I kept the high singsong voice flowing, he seemed to even relax and look around for fallen birdseed. That was my cue. I scattered seed near him and then closer and closer to me. Perhaps over the months he has studied me enough to know that I am the seed-giver.

That was yesterday and today the saga continues with even greater results. My new prospective friend returns and we replay our dance. This time he comes so close I could reach out and stroke his marvelous silky fur coat. Just as I begin to feel familiar with my becoming-friend, another appears and confuses me. The same fur design is identically replicated in this new companion (or adversary?) that comes into our drama. How will I tell them apart? I am quite observant but can find no distinguishing markings. Spoken like a true human, "they all look alike!" I am sure that another chipmunk could immediately point out the differences. But if we are going to be friends, I will just have to find his uniqueness.

I do know that this chipmunk is possessive, aggressive, and territorial. Here we are, having a wonderful time getting acquainted, and he lets the new chipmunk distract him over and over – running away, chasing him away from his private bird seed stash. Can't he see there is more than enough for both of them? Doesn't he know that the magical garbage can holds enough birdseed to feed both of them forever? Each time I scatter seed, he scoots around the porch like a mini vacuum cleaner, filling his cheeks full to bursting. Then he disappears down the hole and reappears with flattened cheeks and little paws that repeatedly clean off his nose.

All of a sudden, the chipmunk pauses and listens carefully to a strange call in the distance. I hear it too and try to discern the source. Is it an animal? A bird? We both sit still and rigid in careful attention when suddenly a hawk lands on the tree twenty-five feet away.

What will I do if it attacks my chipmunk friend? Will I intervene or, out of respect for nature, will I let the drama take its course? Knowing me, I'm afraid my loyal-friend-reflex will take over. Fortunately neither of us is put to the test. The hawk has disappeared into the tall hemlock in the distance.

For the past five minutes, the chipmunk, with cheeks filled to overflowing, sends out the strangest call. It is loud and relentless. It sounds like a ping-pong tournament. I could be very wrong, but he appears to be on an important vocal mission. Still at attention, he seems quite unconcerned that I am near enough to touch him, as I too am still "at attention" and somewhat in awe of the hawk visitation. His call goes out like a warning to the other creatures and perhaps to the other chipmunk who is nowhere in sight.

Like humans protecting their turf, this chipmunk seems to have nothing but disdain for his competitor. Yet, when faced with the threat of a common enemy, do I detect a hint of loyalty? Like a fussy old married couple that has settled into a habit of bickering, yet bristles if anyone else shows the other disrespect, perhaps these chipmunks are loyal too.

ROBIN RADAR

The robins are avidly scanning our property for worms. They have captured my attention as their eating process fascinates me. They hop around the yard, taking long attentive pauses. They do this repeatedly until they finally pierce the ground with their beaks. Then they magically retract it with a worm attached. From what I can tell, they don't hit or miss but only pierce the ground when they have a fairly sure catch. I am noticing an astounding success rate.

What in the world is going on during those pauses? Are they actually hearing the worms? Are they getting an inner feeling or a "discernment?" Are they getting a message from the Robin Radar Tower? I can't imagine! All I know is that they are incredibly precise in their aim and are able to locate a huge number of worms in a very short time.

Indigenous people would say that these birds have "inner vision," another way of knowing that all creatures have. Early on, humans relied on this "knowing within" as it guided their survival. It is this inner vision that enabled them to distinguish between edible plants and poisonous plants. It guided them to medicinal plants and their usage. It helped them decipher their path in the wilderness.

We call this inner vision "intuition," but when it is very well developed, we no longer consider it a normal faculty. Those in whom it is well developed are given honor, or in some circles, are demonized. Some would say that this inner knowing is the voice of God. I would not disagree with them. However, "inner vision" will never be trapped in a particular religion or denomination or doctrine. This "knowing within" is with each culture, each race, and each living being. It is this place within that sustains our collective life and the life of our planet, and indigenous people would say that ignoring it has gone hand in hand with our destruction of the earth.

So perhaps robins really are pausing to listen to their inner messenger. The crucial piece seems to be the attentive listening posture. What would happen if that listening posture were a normal part of human actions and interactions? Perhaps we would foresee the consequences of our impulses. Perhaps we would fathom another's pain instead of increasing it. Perhaps we would widen our circle of concern to include other's needs and not just our own. Maybe we would become creative, seeking alternatives to win/lose or have/have not. Perhaps we would discern a way to live that secures the future for at least the next "seven generations."

NATURE LOVER?

I am a pathetic excuse for a nature lover. I don't love nature at all. Right now I feel like I hate it! It is cruel and it is harsh and it is unfair. I am so angry that I can't get past my upset. I cannot get used to the whole idea of "survival of the fittest." In fact it doesn't seem like "survival of the fittest" but rather "dominance of the most aggressive" or "dominance of the biggest bully" or "death to the most vulnerable." If I were a true nature lover, I would have accepted this situation long ago and I would be able to "go with the flow" as they say! We all have to eat to stay alive, but killing to eat still feels like violent cruel murder to me.

Today I watched my dear frog friend get eaten by the garter snake. It is one thing to know they get eaten and to awaken to one less frog in the frog count, but it is a totally different thing to stand by helplessly and watch a frog friend get eaten. I was furious and still am. The frogs seem so vulnerable and helpless. Our pond is very small, perhaps twenty square feet, and the snakes are not the least bit reluctant to go right in the pond. Where are the frogs supposed to hide? What is their nature-given defense?

Today was the first really hot day and I was not surprised to see the garter snake scanning the pond. I couldn't help myself. I took a big stick and guided the snake away from the pond. Whenever I turned my back it slithered right back there. So I decided I would create a frog sanctuary and would train the snakes to hunt somewhere else. I sat within eight feet of the pond, and every time the snake approached I gently redirected it away from the pond.

I can't figure out how the snake managed to sneak up on not only the frog, but on me as well. I never saw its approach, but I did see it bite the foot of the frog and drag it from the pond. In my panic, I grabbed the stick and tried to separate the snake from the frog. There was no chance. It had an incredibly firm grip on the frog and was not the least bit willing to release its grip. So many thoughts swirled in my head. Should I kill the snake? Absolutely not, it had every right to live. Should I keep persisting in separating them? Probably not as the frog would be very wounded and prime target for the next hit. Perhaps the snake had even poisoned it somehow. My hope was that the snake would eat the frog quickly so that it wouldn't suffer. But it didn't! It dragged the frog into the leaves where they were clearly tussling. At one point I could even see the frog looking up in my direction.

I can't convey the sorrow and the rage I felt in that moment. To be honest, the rage was greater than the sorrow. I was just furious at that big old snake bully. Somehow I couldn't see another needy creature that was hungry after long months hibernating. All I could see was a predator dominating a vulnerable victim. Last time I looked, it was sunning itself with a big fat belly.

Now there is one frog left in the pond and I don't know what to do. Part of me wants to relocate it to a safer pond or at least a bigger one where it might have a better chance of survival. In fact I am ready to pull out the pond and replace it with flowers. I will do my research and figure out if it is a normal situation for green frogs or if it is just a frog trap, a stock pond for snakes. I hate this whole big arrangement – everything eats something else. And to top it all off, a huge spider just crawled down the front of my shirt and scared the heck out of me. All this time I thought I loved nature. Really I love creatures and I love trees and I love beauty. But the ways of nature have left me livid. I found it agonizing to watch it die slowly. Did that frog have some kind of numbing grace? As I look back on my own times of intense suffering, I see the grace that helped me get through. I don't know how to love nature or how to love Life itself without somehow banking on that grace for all.

But my story doesn't end here. I contacted two people who know a lot about nature and creatures. My pressing question remained. "Is the small artificial frog pond a trap or is it natural enough that they have a reasonable amount of normal self-protection?" The feedback concurred. The pond is too small to provide the frog with its natural defense. In nature a pond or creek would be big enough for the frog to swim away and find places to hide from a snake. The pond is too small and too brightly lit for it to have any chance to evade an enemy. My worst fear was confirmed. All the frogs that visit our pond could become an easy meal. I knew what I had to do. I had to remove the snake or remove the pond. For the time being, I chose to move the snake. We very carefully relocated it to a beautiful wooded fifty-acre campground about a mile away. The lone frog is now croaking again, trying to lure a new mate. But my search is not over. I must keep other snakes away or resign myself to getting rid of this artificial pond. It has been the source of endless awe and delight for many of us as I am often told it is exceptionally lovely. I need a little more time before I can rip it out, as it will really feel like ripping out a little piece of my heart. I will do it if it is truly best for the frogs, but I will wait and observe a little longer. I will see if other snakes arrive soon.

So here I am revisiting the same old lesson. Love means letting go. Over and over I am faced with that lesson – so often, loving means letting go. I have had to let go of my parents, my children, my youth, and now I may have to let go of frog friends so that they can thrive in a better environment. I will do my research and my homework, and when I am clear, I will do what love requires, as I do love these frogs and will not betray them.

THE FOX

There was a fox living under my art studio. I didn't invite him, but I am so glad he came. His arrival blessed my studio, my art, and me. Red foxes each have a territory of about two miles. That means that the fox could have picked any of the other trees or sheds or holes that fill this richly wooded countryside, but he didn't. He picked my studio and I have to wonder why. Was he sent to inspire me and fill my art studio with his precious spirit so that my creative juices don't run dry? He has only made his appearance twice. Both were on days when I was at work on a new project that had to be completed quickly.

The first day he noisily arose from his slumber causing me to wonder if I had a raccoon under my flooring. With eyes still shut, he clumsily sauntered within three feet of my window and proceeded to stretch and avidly shake out his wet and matted fur. Gradually his eyes opened, as he looked right at me, not with fear, but as if to say, "What are you doing in my house?" Where was his fear? Why wasn't he acting like the sneaky fox we all envision? All I know is that he pranced toward the creek with the gait of one who had no cares in the world, stopping only to lift his leg and sprinkle the soil.

Weeks later he graced me with the sight of his presence one more time, so as to assure me that this was not all in my imagination. Again he awakened as I was putting the finishing touches on that same project. Again he arose from slumber and checked in the window. I watched with the delight of one about to be reunited with an old friend. Again he sauntered off as if forgetting he was a sly reticent fox.

I haven't seen him since. My art project is complete now and I am guessing his mission is too. And now I am left wondering. How do normal people create art without the support of their wild animal coach? Perhaps they don't!

CHIP-MONKS

It is early summer and the earth is doing what it does best. It is replenishing itself. Our yard has been decorated with a bazillion maple seedpods. They have been clustered on the maples for weeks, but suddenly, in one synchronized event, they take flight. They fall to the ground in one brief twirl of a ride. Will any of them actually take root and become a grand maple? The chances are very slim around our house, but in the woods, some will grow as others die off.

Meanwhile they have obscured any view of the water lilies in the pond or of the seedlings in the garden. Like flower petals decorating the aisle for a bride, these seedpods cover all our walkways and trails. For me they are becoming a nuisance, but for the chipmunks, they are gifts from heaven. They are scurrying around the yard from one to the next, eating the seeds inside the pod with great fervor. They no longer wait for birdseed to drop from the feeder. These chipmunks are in their glory. They have been inundated with more treats than any could eat in several lifetimes.

I love watching the earth lavish such abundance on these small creatures. I love to imagine climbing inside their world, their bliss. Is their world as simple and uncomplicated as it appears? No need to decide how to eat in a manner that is healthy, just, environmentally sound, and economical all at once. No need to think about how to live with a minimal environmental impact. No need to juggle work, family, friends, exercise, spiritual practice, community service, and creative pursuits! No need to wade through contradictory beliefs and values. No need to discern fact from hype in the media. No need to find ones "true self" or "life purpose."

These chipmunks truly live in the "Now" that all spiritual masters espouse. They seem to be entirely focused on the task at hand. I wonder if I have ever eaten anything with the intensity and passion they devote to each seedpod. I would have to stop the inner or outer chatter to do so. I imagine that is why monks eat in silence – to be fully present. Now I have a new icon. Icons are historically understood as windows into God or portals through which one glimpses Divinity. Each year when the seed pods form on the maples, each year as they choose one windy day to take flight, I will remember the chip-monks who eat with passion. I will remember the chip-monks who live in the Now.

AIR SHOW

I didn't understand all that was going on when I first sat down in our open field. All I knew was that an exquisitely radiant blue-green dragonfly was putting on an air show. I'm sure it was a "she" as her dance was so graceful. And her glistening attire was as iridescent as the raku tiles I just fired in my kiln. She was very large, as far as dragonflies go, with at least a four-inch wingspan.

I was mesmerized by her performance. My head rotated back and forth as I watched her fly in huge circles and occasional figure eights. It seemed she would almost fly right into me, but then would suddenly circle back into her pattern. After a few moments of devoted admiration, it dawned on me that miniscule bugs were flying throughout the same space and she was having her lunch in flight. What a delightful arrangement! She not only had the privilege of soaring through fresh fragrant air on the sunniest of our new spring days, but she was served a midair bug buffet as well. What pure bliss! I can just imagine soaring through the air with sandwiches suspended from treetops, or ice cream sundaes floating on air pockets and chocolate sauce dripping into the mouths of those who pass underneath.

Her flight show must have gone on for a good ten minutes without any rest stops. In fact it was I who interrupted the show to grab pencil and paper. Soon after I returned, I was stunned by yet another's flight. Within fifteen feet, a hawk glided past me. I know where it was headed – right to the birdfeeder where it often finds lunch as well. It is not the seed it eats, but rather the seedeaters! It likes chickadees, juncos – whatever!

Today I am more at peace with that. I cannot deny that the same Hand of Life that provides for the dragonfly is providing for the hawk. I cannot celebrate with one and begrudge the other. It is easier to watch the dragonflies eat, as I am less connected to the bugs they consume. I am so connected to the chickadees, though, and hate to see them get killed and eaten. But I will do my best to celebrate the Life that holds them all. In this moment, the glory of this brightest sun seems to pronounce beneficence on all around. So I will soar with the dragonfly in the fullness of the present, knowing that at any moment, she too may become another's lunch. And I will soar, knowing that in an instant, I could be returned to the earth as well.

I will not waste any more time begrudging that which is so hard to understand. This moment is too delicious. The air is so sensuous, and the earth is so pregnant with aromas and textures and colors that are about to burst into the extravagance of full-blown spring. Somehow this dragonfly heralds perfection, and for now, puts all my quandaries to rest.

NATURE-WATCHING

As I walk past my window, I see a convention of juncos. Juncos are gray birds with light gray bellies, and prefer to eat from the ground. Something on our lawn has captivated them and they are arriving ten at a time. As I count, the numbers rise from fifty to one hundred or more. Obviously there is something very special hidden in that grass. All I see is endless pecking. Each junco has about a six-inch turf and no trespassing!

I am fascinated by this unusual event. As I grab my binoculars, I search for an explanation. My mind leaps to a movie I saw about a couple in New York City throwing dollar bills out the window of a tall building. They loved to watch the frenzy as people competed for the money. The scene before me is similar. These juncos have received "manna from heaven" and are clearly enraptured. As I watch intently, suddenly they all disperse in a panic. One of them actually crashes into my window. (Fortunately we leave the screens on all year so they won't hit the glass.) I look around for an explanation. A hawk? A loud noise? I see nothing. I hear nothing. Another mystery!

Once again, I realize that the wonder of nature has lured me away from my duties. All day long, I could stand at the window or sit under a tree just watching! That is what I often did as a child, and I was rarely bored. There is so much going on in the natural world all the time. It is so much more fascinating than television or computers. How tragic that such a huge gift has been swapped for technology and cyber-reality.

Some say they want to learn to connect with nature. I appreciate their intent, but perhaps it is not something to "learn." Isn't it rather something that has been forgotten? Maybe the connection to nature is like a deeply buried memory that unfolds as it is given time and space. We know how to relish the mystery of humans and human behavior. Doesn't everyone love to people-watch at a sidewalk café? We can linger the same way in nature. We can tree-watch or bug-watch or cloud-watch. Any of them will bring us into the Great Mystery. Any time spent respectfully watching and appreciating nature brings us back. It brings us to our truest selves, our most gentle selves – our most childlike selves. That is nature's gift to us. It brings us home.

THE BEETLE

The sun porch has been in need of sweeping for several days. Suddenly, I feel the need to sweep it, now! I grab the broom and begin the task. At the end, in the last corner, I notice a beetle upside down - flailing its legs in the air. It is stuck. There is no way for it to right itself. I grab the dustpan, slide the beetle on, walk outside and pour it into the garden. It lands on its back but is able to right itself. I notice the brilliance of its back and the delicacy of its legs. I'm glad it didn't die. I am glad it will live to enjoy the beauty of this day.

A bible passage comes to mind. "Not one sparrow can fall to the ground without your Father knowing it." I must translate:
"Not one beetle can get stuck on its back without the Source of All Life knowing."

I am struck with a sense that this verse is entirely true. I am convinced that I was inspired to sweep at that moment. It feels true to my core that the Giver of Life really cares enough about that beetle to send help. I don't know why that kind of help doesn't always come to everyone and everything, every time. I just don't know. I have spent endless hours, days, weeks and months trying to understand that mystery to no avail. It remains a mystery.

But I do know that the Source of Love cares about each life. Yes, even a bug. That reminder humbles me. Recently I have been fretting about my life course – or lack of clear course. I have been feeling a bit lost, without guidance from the heavens. I have been a bit overwhelmed by the complexity and challenge of reinventing my life at this stage. And now, I am given a mere beetle as my messenger this day.

My life is known, seen, and guided in every moment by One who breathed me into existence. My life is not a tapestry of random events, but is being woven with love and care by One who watches over even little beetles. Fretting is what I do when I forget this. But fortunately I am sent messengers regularly - messengers with words and messengers, like beetles, who need no words.

THE SETTLEMENT

It is early morning. A chipmunk neighbor is perched in the bush right by my bedroom window. He is sending out a high-pitched staccato communication. His persistence annoys me. The sound goes on and on. I can't sleep! It is warm outside, but I still shut the window. I crawl back into bed, hoping to pick up where I left off in my dream. I wait for sleep, but it does not come. Now I am getting desperate for rest. I turn on the fan hoping it will drown out the sound.

Eventually I fall back asleep even though the call can still be heard above the droning fan. I sleep enough and awaken to a beautiful day. I open the window and notice the chipmunk is at it again. Or is he still at it? Is he rejoicing in the beautiful weather? Is he calling for a mate? Why on earth does he go on and on this way? Is he trying to drive me crazy? I go about my chores. Finally I pay attention to my sensations. The sound is driving me crazy! It is so insistent, so piercing, and so ever present. This has been going on long enough! Something inside me snaps.

I go outside and follow the sound to its source. The chipmunk is on a low branch in the bush below my window. He doesn't run away. He is used to me now and just stares back at me. I am now only a few feet away. I crouch down and look him in the eye as I speak. I'm not yelling, but there is emotion in my voice. "Your sound is driving me crazy. Do you have to do that right here? Can't you go somewhere else to make your noise? Please?" He stares back at me and stops. I go in the house thinking he will start right back up, but he doesn't. This sound that has been relentlessly long has now stopped. I am shocked. I go in the house and enjoy at least half an hour of silence. I am grateful.

Now I hear the sound again. I go to the window. Yes, it is the chipmunk. Yes, he's at it again. I decide to try one more time. I go back to him and thank him for my half an hour of peace, and then restate my case. "Can't you do this somewhere else? It is so annoying." This time he interrupts. As I speak, he chirps back. Each phrase of mine gets a chirping reply. We are clearly arguing this time, or perhaps I should say we are simply politely negotiating. I go back into the house and am uncertain how this one will pan out. Who won the debate? I am waiting and listening. No sound! I have won this round it seems. I wonder how long it will last?

It is lasting a long time. All I hear now is birdsong. Birds are not annoying. My husband arrives and I tell him my story. He says, "That's neat, you can talk to animals." I wonder if he really believes that or if he is just playing along with me. But I respond, "Ya know, I think anyone probably can."

I really believe the chipmunk and I were communicating. Indigenous people of all cultures have been able to cross the communication barrier that we have erected. They know that all creatures are sentient and have their own means of communicating. There are those who know the language of birds and can decipher their warnings. Even Saint Francis was known to have negotiated a settlement with a wolf that was devastating a village. We have relegated creatures to an inferior category and have made ourselves incapable of penetrating the joy of interspecies communication. Yes, some of us feel we communicate with our domesticated pets, but ancient cultures tell us we can go way beyond that. We can communicate with all life forms. That chipmunk didn't catch my words, but my tone and my body conveyed a message. And who knows how much intuition is at work in all creatures? As Derrick Jensen puts it, there is a "language older than words," and those who dare to speak it are blessed with "more-than-human" friends.

An Affair of the Heart

My husband is gone a great deal these days. He commutes to Detroit for school and will often stay with friends during the week. Being alone in the woods can get a little isolating for me sometimes. But I warned him. I told him that one of these days I'd have to find a boyfriend. And I did!

My boyfriend is rather housebound, so I visit him as often as I can. I know the best way to his heart is through his stomach so I bring him treats regularly. He's the silent mysterious type so I do most of the talking. But I'm learning to be comfortable with the silence between us too. Sometimes it seems we are both listening intently to words neither of us can say. But he stays so attentive to me, it is disarming. In those silent intimate times we speak almost telepathically. Then I caress his head and he nuzzles into my neck, smelling my hair. He sniffs slowly as if noticing each subtle scent, one by one. Sometimes his face brushes against mine as his whiskers skim my cheeks. And other times he remains so near, it is as if his breath merges with my own.

I am undone by the intimacy. It is tempting to back off, but neither of us does. We let the moments unfold and the trust deepen. In the quiet, a million questions seem suspended in the air, and then they dissipate unanswered. They too are unnecessary. I know his love for me is growing. He greets me with abandon now. He runs to the gate to meet me as soon as he glimpses my arrival.

I think it is the silence between us that is the most compelling. We speak with intuition, and I know he can feel my heart. Mostly he can feel my affection and joy, but perhaps he can feel my fear too. I'm just a little bit afraid of him. He seems so strong and powerful, so independent and knowing. I don't think he would purposely hurt me, but like a clumsy kindergartner, unaware of his strength, he could easily injure me inadvertently.

I will admit it, going to visit him is exhilarating and I always return elated. My husband's not the jealous type, but he must sense my heart swelling a bit when I mention my boyfriend. Maybe he's not too jealous because I don't even know his name. It is true. I don't even know my boyfriend's name! But maybe that isn't it at all. Maybe the truth is that my husband's not jealous because he knows my "boyfriend" is a stunning white horse.

WILD TURKEYS

I first noticed the five wild turkeys this past spring. Four of them were babies and one was a very protective and attentive mother. She has done her job well as they are all grown now and are as huge as she. They are actually beautiful creatures in their own way. Their tail feathers form a complex design of intricately crafted patterns that they display while resting in the sun. By day they scavenge with their huge long legs and by night they sleep in the treetops. But they are far from graceful as they ascend, plowing their way through the branches with way too much commotion. This family of five has been on my mind a lot lately. I haven't seen them for days, which is unusual. With the arrival of the hunting season, I have been doing my best to avoid morbid thoughts of their likely destiny. I've also wondered how they would survive the winter. Somehow their absence seems to mirror my struggle with my own family's dispersion.

Two sons have moved to California and the other lives up north with his wife and daughter. Our family has been very close as we share so many similar passions. So I have languished over the likelihood that the holidays will be a challenge, and being united will not be a given. It is hard for me to accept the dispersion of that which I have labored to nurture for twenty-five years. But once again, I am challenged to let go of what was and allow the new to unfold. I heartily believe in that principle, yet it is always easier to know it in my mind than to live it out in my life. So far I have navigated this Thanksgiving with no family around, but with a lovely gathering of peers instead. I am holding my own with hopes for a reunion at Christmas.

Today the first snow of the season beckoned me to the window. It is transforming a dismal gray morning into the loveliest black and white etching. Each twig on our myriad of trees has been underscored with white accents. The beauty is a great consolation for the frigid temperatures of Michigan. Suddenly my eyes catch sight of a big brown batch of feathers under the bird feeder. It is a turkey! I am elated. My first thought as I see another is "Hooray, two of them survived." But as I keep peering further around the corner of the bushes, three more come into view. All five have survived! I call my husband, "Come quickly – it's amazing! All five turkeys survived. The whole family is still together!" I shriek with glee. He runs quickly so he can share in my joy. I can't help but think of it as a sign. Their family has survived the challenges. And ours will too!

DEER DISRUPTION

I awoke this morning to a window filled with six deer resting in the pine needles. What a relief to find they all survived despite the recent persistent sound of hunters coming near. It is so difficult to attend to a day's responsibilities when I could spend all my moments gazing at these gentle creatures.

But I had a meeting to attend so I prepared to leave and glanced when possible. As the morning quickly passed, I grabbed the car keys and made my way via the porch, which is nothing but window walls. In each direction the house was surrounded by deer that were coming closer and closer. Two of them were approaching the bird feeder on my left, two were walking up to the boardwalk that stood between my car and me, and two to the right were wandering into our little flower garden that surrounds the frog pond, not eight feet from the living room window. Large animals never come that close to our home, except our neighbor's gigantic cow that got loose and decided to use our bird feeder pole for a scratching-post! Wondering what they were finding so delicious, I slowly approached the window. I soon discovered it was the myrtle ground cover that grows prolifically in the garden.

These creatures had all morning to wander, but it seems they chose the precise moment I needed to leave to begin their exploration. With car keys still in hand, it was becoming quite clear that I would not be attending the meeting that day. The Deer Festival was literally forming a barricade between my car and me. I could not find it within me to disrupt such an ecstatic event.

As I allowed the moment to alter my plans, my thoughts traveled to another time, another place. I was nineteen years old and living with a family in the French Alps. There on top of the Semnoz mountain range, overlooking Lake Annecy, I could hear the music of cowbells everywhere as each bell made a different melody for its cow. There in my mind's eye were the cows casually crossing the street while the drivers waited patiently. As the waiting line grew longer, some exited their cars to get a better view of the beautifully sunlit panorama. How I long to live in a society where it makes perfect sense to miss a meeting because there are deer at the door, or one where traffic stops for turtles or cows who need to cross the street, or one where airplanes reroute for bird migrations, or one where boats stop for slow- swimming manatee!

THE PAUSE

I have such trouble accepting the drama that unfolded outside my kitchen window today. I awoke to perfection. Five inches of fresh snow became the final white brushstrokes on the canvas of stark maple branches, white pine trees, and thick juniper bushes. The juniper has become the ideal canopy to shelter the wild birds from snow and harsh winter winds. They have easy access to the seed feeders and to a protected refuge close by. Flitting from feeder to refuge and back again, the birds always have plenty of food.

Watching the blissful gathering of cardinals, juncos, nuthatches, titmice, chickadees, and varied woodpeckers, I felt like I was also becoming part of the peaceful, tranquil scene. Then, very suddenly, a strikingly beautiful sharp-shinned hawk seized a little junco. It happened so quickly; all I saw was the stark pattern of tail feathers ascending and a bird in the talons. After the blurry scene, all that remained were the tiny feathers confirming that I really did see what I saw.

The other confirmations were the knot in my stomach and the fact that all the other birds were hidden from view. It was all so fast and harsh. The violence pierced the moment just like the hawk's sharp talons pierced the junco. Where was the warning? Life often omits warnings and gives us shocks instead. Were the other birds shocked? Were they shaken to the core? It didn't seem so. They resumed the dance, flitting back and forth between feeder and juniper bushes. Perhaps it was the urgency of the cold weather that sent them back to business-as-usual so quickly.

But it bothered me. I wanted everything to stop. I wanted the life of that little bird to be commemorated somehow. It was snatched from the dance and now it is no more. It is so very real to me that every bit of life has value. Was its value only in its offering to the hungry hawk?

Perhaps it is the indigenous people of this land who have best understood my conflict. As part of the hunt, they would traditionally pause and offer gratitude for the animal's sacrifice. It is part of the design that all would eat and be eaten, but it is that pause that I need. I need a pause that says, "Yes, we will go back to business as usual, but not without gratitude for the sacrifices that are constantly given so that others might live."

GROUNDHOG DAY

It is February 2nd today…Groundhog Day! According to the legend, if the groundhog emerges from hibernation and sees its shadow, it will be frightened back into its hole, "presaging six more weeks of winter." But if it is a cloudy day with no shadow, the winter will end early, so they say.

I'm particularly drawn to this legend this year because we have a special groundhog that is sharing our turf. We met this groundhog, or "woodchuck" as it is also called, last fall. Well, we didn't exactly meet, but we learned to share our land in a respectful manner. I don't know if it was ignoring us or just didn't see us, but it regularly spent time as close to our house as one can get without walking right on in. In fact one day it sat on the porch and stared right in the glass door. I managed to restrain myself from opening it.

Another day, while resting in the hammock, I watched the groundhog go back and forth across our driveway carrying mouthfuls of crunchy leaves. It carefully deposited them under the front porch steps for at least half an hour. This groundhog was totally focused on preparing for the winter dwelling and was not about to let me deter it.

Other days it sat on our boardwalk stuffing its fat belly with little apples that fell from our trees. Somehow this fat furry creature reminded me more of a cute little bear than of a rodent. But from what I've heard, these groundhogs are not as harmless as they look and can be quite aggressive. So I kept a respectful distance.

Now as I sit by the wood-burning stove, I imagine our groundhog neighbor sleeping under the porch only twenty feet away. I see it curled up in all those leaves it collected so diligently. I wonder if it came out today to look around and then retreat for another stint below. I don't know. I didn't see it, nor did I see sunshine and shadows. So I like the suggestion that winter will end early this year.

More than that, I like the thought that we are waiting together, the groundhog and I. I like the feeling of being in sync with an animal relation who also awaits the sun and warmth. I like the idea of literally sharing the structure of this house with a wild creature that needs warmth. And I love the thought it will wait with us for the greenery to return.

So as I sit and stare at the floor, twenty feet in front of me, I pretend I have x-ray vision and can look through to the nest below. I see a contented groundhog resting in the leaves, and I too feel restful and still. I tell myself it is okay to wait and to rest. It is good to hibernate sometimes and to pause for "time out." It is right and good to let things germinate and come to fruition in their own time. And it is good and right to do that together, animals and humans. Together!

SANCTUARY

I am totally enjoying one of those rare phone conversations where I can leisurely talk with our son Daniel who is an Episcopal priest. We are discussing the sermon he is about to deliver. As we ponder the ins and outs of law and grace, our conversation is interrupted by the appearance of a sharp-shinned hawk at my window. As the bird surveys our bird feeder, my end of the conversation totally loses its course.

"Daniel, there's a hawk near the birdfeeder!" I announce with tension in my voice.

"That's cool," he responds.

"No, it's not," I quickly reply. "He is going to eat one of the birds and they are like my friends."

"Well, is he one of your friends too? He needs food too and has to eat meat to survive."

"I guess you are right," I reply with resignation in my voice.

By now the hawk is pursuing a chickadee. The chickadee weaves in and out of juniper bushes to evade him. For the moment the chickadee is successful.

"I feel like I have created a feeding station for predators just by feeding the birds. And my fish and frog pond as well – all I am doing is getting the frogs plump for the snakes to eat in the spring," I add venting all my woes.

"Well Mom, you don't allow people to hunt deer on your property. In a way, your land really is a creature sanctuary. The birds need a sanctuary too," he reflects.

"Do you think so?" I ask with hope rising.

"Uh huh! I think you should ask the hawk to hunt someplace else."

"Really Daniel? You mean actually talk to him?" I ask naively.

"Try it!" he urges.

With the cordless phone still in my hand, I slide the glass door open. The hawk moves away but not far enough. He is lingering high in the treetops.

"Nah! He's not going anywhere. He is just surveying from on high," I whine.

"Mom, just try it. Ask him," he repeats quite firmly.

I look into the treetops and ask him calmly, "Would you please go hunting somewhere else?" I'm definitely feeling a bit silly by now. But within seconds, I am reporting with glee,

"He is leaving Daniel. The hawk is flying far away. I can't even see him any more. He is gone now. That's crazy! I think it really worked." We are both laughing now.

We hang up the phone and go back to our separate days. I look outside. The birds are resuming their day as well. They are coming out of hiding and are back at the feeder.

I go to the dictionary and look up the word sanctuary. It says,
"A holy place. A place of refuge or protection. A reservation where animals or birds are sheltered."

Our home – a holy place – a place of refuge and protection, I like the sound of that!

INNER GUIDANCE

It was a normal frigid winter morning in Michigan as I prepared to walk to my studio in the woods. The studio is perched on our hill overlooking the hardwood forest and winding creek. It was also a normal moment when an inner voice clearly said, "Bring your binoculars with you." For some people, inner voices can be momentous, but for me they are usually pretty ordinary, like "bring your umbrella" or "call your sister." I often ignore that voice and later regret it, but on rare occasions, I have listened and been grateful that I did. This was one of those occasions. I must admit, there was something playful and almost feisty in my response though. "Okay, I will listen, but this better be for a good reason or I won't be so quick to respond next time." Grabbing the binoculars, almost defiantly, I headed to my studio.

I hadn't been working long before I found my eyes wandering out the window. They scanned all the familiar spots like the creek in the distance where deer sometimes drink, or the nearby hole where the fox lives. Nothing seemed unusual. So having finally forgotten about the binoculars, it was the commotion of a large flock of birds that diverted my attention. They clustered around the huge hemlock tree nearly thirty feet in front of me. I began squinting, trying hard to identify the species. Were they cedar waxwings? I couldn't see well so I grabbed the binoculars.

As they came into perfect view, I was shocked! In the middle of a frigid Michigan winter, I was looking at birds one would only expect to see in the Caribbean. The males were bright pink, not red, but truly pink. My mind scanned all the usual possibilities, but they were clearly not purple finches or anemic cardinals. I had never seen this bird, ever! I knew enough to look carefully for distinguishing markings, and did notice two white wing bars and the fact that they fled from one hemlock to the next. With a backdrop of stark white snow, these brilliantly bright pink birds were exquisitely beautiful. I was transported to memories of Tobago where tropical birds sat on our teacups and long-tailed mot-mots perched several feet away. In a dismal long gray winter, the arrival of bright pink visitors is nothing short of miraculous. It all happened so quickly, I was breathless with excitement as they left as fast as they arrived.

I soared back to the house, grabbed the bird book, and began looking for confirmation that there was in fact such an unusual bird. I quickly found what I had seen as it was so unique, but the birds were more pink than the photo conveyed. I later learned that this bird is most intensely pink during the winter season. The book revealed that the visitors were white-winged crossbills. They are very "uncommon and irregular" in our region but they definitely prefer hemlock trees and do travel exclusively in groups. My next search was on line where I learned that this unique bird had recently been seen in other parts of Michigan. I was totally thrilled to be one of those graced by their presence. As I sauntered back to my studio, reveling in the joy of the encounter, I felt a bit awestruck. What if I had not listened to the urging within? If I had not had the binoculars, I would have entirely missed the experience. The binoculars were my entryway into a world that was otherwise out of reach.

How many times have I ignored that inner voice? How many other experiences were never born because I so easily slide past those inner leadings? I got the message this time and a deep resolve has begun. I will listen from now on. I will heed the voice within even when it seems silly or pointless. And I will remain thankful to the One who sends the messages. I believe it was the "Spirit-that-moves-through-all-things," but you never know. It could be any number of heavenly agents like my own personal angel. But then again, my husband had his own take on it. As we were lying in bed discussing our days, I said,
"Richard, I wonder who exactly told me to bring the binoculars today. What do you think?"
He immediately replied, "It was Handel." Handel is one of my very favorite composers so I loved playing with that idea.
"Handel? Why do you say Handel?"
"Because he loved nature," he answered.
"Really?" I responded with excitement that my beloved composer might have loved nature as much as I do.

Richard has returned to school later in life to study music so I entirely believed him when he said Handel loved nature. But the next day I learned that Richard had no recollection of our conversation. We figured out that he had, in fact, been sleep-talking. I should have known. But he did concede that, according to his studies, Handel very well could have been a nature lover, as Baroque composers often idealized nature in their music. So it remains a mystery. To whom shall I send my gratitude for the message to bring my binoculars? I will remain thankful to the Giver of Life for gifting all of us with the amazing ability to receive inner guidance. But secretly I will always wonder, was it really Handel who whispered in my ear?

FEATHERS

I've been picking up feathers in the woods since I was a little girl. I can even remember my first show and tell in kindergarten. I came with a dragonfly wing, some rocks, a partial blue robin's egg and some feathers, my most precious possessions. All I remember is disappointment that others didn't seem to fully appreciate my treasures.

There are feathers throughout my home. I have big ones from wild turkeys, bright yellow ones from yellow-shafted flickers, blue ones from jays, and today I added junco feathers to the collection. Junco feathers are small and gray and not particularly noticeable until you pick one up. They are so fine and delicate, one can see right through them. In fact they could almost be mistaken for a dragonfly wing.

I am awed by the world of details. So many feel that we must explore the expanses of outer space in order to expand our view. But I don't think we have even begun to fathom the miracle of inner space, up close space, or micro space. One of my favorite activities is to take a child into nature with a magnifying glass. Roping off one square foot of earth, you invite the child to go exploring in the close-up jungle. There are so many worlds inside any square foot of nature. There is the world of insect civilizations, or the world of microscopic details imprinted on each blade of grass, or the world of light prisms reflected in each drop of dew. I have never seen a child grow bored with this exercise. And they always return with stories to tell.

I too am never bored when planted in nature. In fact "planted" is the key word. When I remain still and quiet in one spot, nature comes and unfolds around me. I begin to notice things that others miss when passing quickly. Those are the only times I am bored, when hurrying from vista to vista in order to catch another panorama. It is often hard to be still, but I know no greater reward than that of being still enough for a wild animal to come near or for a simple junco feather to reveal its glory.

DISABILITIES

Today I awaken to my favorite gift. As I pull up the shade, two deer appear within thirty feet of my window. There is perfection in the beauty of the view before me. The day is brightly lit by an unbroken blue sky. The deer are under the white pines that are not white at all, but very green. The vibrant red clusters of sumac accent the ten inches of stark white snow that envelops the scene.

There is no movement except for the one lone black squirrel who is doing his best to navigate the snow. I assume he will jump through the many inches of light snow. Instead he holds his head straight up as if surveying the sky, and keeping it that way, rapidly plows through the snow with the force of his body. He must be quite relieved as he arrives at the tree trunk that takes him to the byways of easy treetop travel.

Suddenly the smaller deer rises. He is perfect in his form and his thick lustrous fur is indicative of good health. In contrast his mother rises and she is wobbly and unsteady. I notice her leg is severed above her knee. I would bet my life savings, that a car or a gun injured her leg. I just can't get used to that!

As I watch her struggle, Jim's words from yesterday echo in my mind. Jim has an injured back and lives with pain that comes and goes. Yesterday the pain was very intense. When I offered him empathy, his response was simple and matter of fact. "We all have disabilities." I think he was lovingly addressing my struggle with my voice. I have a vocal cord condition that causes my voice to crack.

I am watching this deer very carefully as she lives with a severe disability. She is so beautiful and resilient as she continues to live her life caring for the younger deer. Her will-to-live outweighs her struggle. She is managing and even seems well adjusted to being on three legs. As she looks around, it seems she is also scanning the beauty of this day. She is a messenger to me, and a role model as well. I feel her dignity and her courage.

She is limping through life with attentiveness to the beauty, devotion to the younger deer, and a seeming confidence that her needs will be provided. Perhaps that is all I need to remember in this life. Accept that "we all have disabilities." Be attentive to extravagant beauty in the natural world. Move forward with confidence that everything needed will be provided, and be ever mindful of those who are younger or weaker.

THE SONG OF CREATION

Spring is just beginning, but it is warm and the sky is as blue as the glacial waters of the Canadian Rockies. Only the most intrepid flowers have begun to appear, and the dry brown leaves still hug the ground, protecting it from recent frost. As I bask in the sun's radiance, I am struck by the stillness. There is so little movement. Everything is resting and relaxing in the warmth of this day. This is such a sharp contrast to the intensity of winter. It was a brutal winter: harsh winds, endless snowfall, large branches torn from trees, and nonstop noisy snowplows. It was a winter filled with the commotion of coping.

But all is still now. The branches are barely moving and the birds are unusually quiet. It feels like the silence just before someone says something very important, or the silence in a noisy room after someone speaks softly. Suddenly the noise ceases and everyone listens attentively, so not to miss the soft words that may be special. I am listening attentively as well. I am leaning forward, almost straining to hear what the earth is saying. This silence is full of mystery and blessing. I want to get the message. I feel it, but I want the words that go with the feelings. The feeling is pure gentleness. I want to catch the words that are floating on the air. I don't want to make them up in my imagination. I want to discern what nature is truly saying. So I am listening. I feel a grand smile returned to me and the only words that come are "All is Well."

I know that is not a personal message but rather a commentary on the state of Mother Earth. But how can that be? All is well? We know that all is not well! Never has this earth been so badly abused. Never has our own survival as a species been in such jeopardy. If all is well, then it is a wellness that is so immense I cannot grasp it: a wellness assured by the earth's ability to regenerate, a wellness that surpasses our human ability to destroy, a wellness that assures me that the Giver of Life holds the final trump card.

Hopi Indians say that humans have seen three other worlds on earth and are now in the fourth one. One world ended with massive fighting, one ended with the ice age, and the other ended with a great flood, they say. We have failed three previous experiments of humanity. They tell us that the conditions for survival in our world are simple, but we have forgotten the "Original Instructions."

We must remember to sing the "Song of Creation." If we are faithful to do so, we can stay in this beautiful world. What exactly is the "Song of Creation?" The Hopi teach that different races of humanity come from the four corners of the earth. They say that someday we will all unite, remembering our Creator and the web that connects us. They tell us it is through the power of the song all colors and races were created. It is through the power of the song that we will endure if we remember to sing it with all our hearts.

Maybe that is what I sense in this gentle stillness – the "Song of Creation." Perhaps that is our hope. If we are very still and attentive, we will be able to hear the "Song of Creation" and sing it with all our hearts.

CHIPMUNK RENDEZVOUS

I have a chipmunk friend who eats birdseed from my hand. I haven't seen him all winter since he hibernates, but it is spring now and he is back. I love to rest on the porch steps and watch the beauty unfold. That was our agreed upon feeding spot last fall, and he seems to remember. My arrival on the porch gets him all excited. When I sit there I see him scurrying around, as if awaiting the treats. So I perch on the top step and sprinkle a few seeds on the bottom step. He joins me almost immediately. He quickly mounts the stairs, rushes past my feet and then jumps to the top step where my open hand is resting, filled with sunflower seeds. Without hesitation, he begins to eat from my hand. His cheeks begin to fill until they are bulging with seeds that he will store in his nearby hole.

The greatest thrill is feeling his soft paws curling around my fingers as he eats. And his relatively huge black eyes occasionally look my way. But mostly he focuses on filling his cheeks to overflowing. He seems absolutely fearless and intrepid. I am the only one who can feel a little bit afraid. My mother's voice lingers behind a nearby tree saying, "Nancy, what if he bites you, he could have rabies!" Her voice is so annoying. I do my best not to let it interfere. Of course I know she could be right, but if I catered to her fear, I would never have any fun. And having a chipmunk eat from your hand is grand fun!

My mother loved my sister and me passionately and was a bit overly protective. Perhaps she couldn't bear the thought of losing us like she lost some of her siblings when they were young. But if I heeded her voice, I wouldn't feed the chipmunks, I wouldn't ride my new electric scooter down the back country roads, and I wouldn't do anything that could result in physical harm.

Fortunately my mother never tried to protect us from emotional harm. She never said, "Nancy, don't fall in love, you might get hurt." She knew it is worth taking a risk in order to live life to the fullest. She never encouraged me to build walls with others, and I usually don't. I have learned that walls do not really protect from hurt. The walls actually increase the hurt. Only true vulnerability, offered in appropriate settings, protects relationships. I have learned that putting down emotional weapons and sharing honest feelings allows relationships to be renewed and healed.

Tomorrow my husband and I will celebrate thirty-five years of marriage, and I am so grateful for these principles that have helped sustain us. We have not been without rough moments, but we have navigated them with forgiveness and renewed vulnerability. I don't know how many more years we will have together, but I pray we will live them fearlessly and with an abandonment to love.

When it comes to love, I have no illusions about the chipmunk. I know he doesn't love me per se, but rather loves my sunflower seeds. But I love him! I love the connection he gives me to another world. I love the suggestion of a world where animals and humans live together harmoniously. The Judeo-Christian scriptures say there will be a time when "the lion and the lamb will lie down together." I don't know if that image is figurative or predictive, but I thoroughly love it and in it I find my deepest joy.

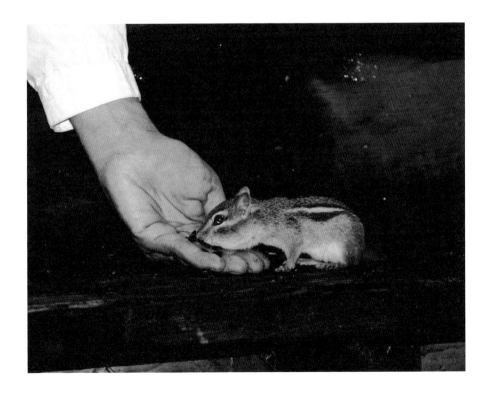

WOODCHUCK FOOD

I suspected it was the woodchuck that had been devastating my perennial garden, but today I caught him in the act. I've carefully chosen perennials to surround the small pond near the house. The lilies do well and the ferns are prolific, but the blossoms on the columbine get devoured upon arrival. This morning there were ten pink flowers hanging upside down. Now there are only four. I caught him just as he was shoving them in his face.

I flew to the window and prepared to clink on the glass with my ring. I knew that piercing sound would scare him off. But I stopped abruptly. I couldn't do it. I couldn't scare him away. I think I was just too curious and wanted to see just exactly how he operates. But the longer I watched, the more he cast a spell over me. He is so darn endearing. He sits on his hind legs looking as cute as a cuddly stuffed teddy bear in a baby's crib. He was having so much fun. Then he grabbed the fluffy yellow flowers and stuffed them all over his face like a lady powdering her nose. He checked out the daisies that aren't quite ready. I have no doubt they are next on the menu.

I'm not sure what happened in those short moments between wanting to scare him away and wanting to cuddle him. I imagine it was stepping back, resisting the urge to control, and then appreciating the moment as it was. And I really did enjoy it! I had so much vicarious pleasure identifying with the woodchuck's lusty lunch that I was giggling. Then he sauntered away from the pond, nibbling parsley and nasturtium along the way.

This year I decided to do an experiment. The plan was to plant wildflowers and perennials and then learn which ones are distasteful to woodchucks. Then the next year I could plant the "distasteful" ones exclusively. So this year the woodchuck and I are "sharing." At first I would get angry at all he ate. Now I am learning to appreciate what he leaves behind. I'm noticing he never eats an entire plant. He always leaves enough greenery so the plant can survive. I don't know if he is being considerate or just plain smart. He will have enough for tomorrow if he restrains himself today.

How basic is that principle? And yet we humans can't seem to get it! Many try to tell me we are smarter than animals. I just don't see it that way. How smart is it to kill the planet that sustains us? No other creature does that!

I think my woodchuck friend and I will be able to work out a mutually acceptable arrangement. I won't have to kill him or poison him with nasty chemicals. I won't have to build fences everywhere. I will just learn how to coexist with him. And I will plant enough for both of us. So once again, there is that lingering question. Whose yard is it anyway?

NAMING OR NOT

I am counting the chipmunks as they scavenge for fallen birdseeds. There are five but my favorite is not around. That would be the one with an eye missing. Why is that one my favorite? Because I can relate to her imperfections? Partly! But it is also because we have a history and I can distinguish her from the others. She was one of the first to eat from my hand and I have watched her change over time. Her eye was once her only distinction, but now her front right arm has shriveled up and disappeared as well. Despite having only one eye and three legs, she seems to function quite well. She doesn't put up with others who would exploit her weakness and will chase and scuffle like the rest.

As I watch, I realize that distinguishing her from the rest gives me a sense of bondedness with her. This might explain the need to name animals. In some farm communities, parents do not allow their children to name the animals that will be butchered. They know that if they name them, they will learn to love them and then agonize over their eventual slaughter. It is hard to eat one you have named and loved. Their logic makes sense.

Yet I am fascinated with a different view. The author, Jim Corbett, arrives at the opposite conclusion. In his book, *Sanctuary for All Life*, he says, " I avoid eating anything I haven't known and cherished." During his life he was utterly committed to the welfare of the animals on his land. When it came time to eat one of them, he knew they had lived well and died as humanely as possible. He was grateful for their sacrifice. He also believed that the way we eat is key to realigning our planet with justice. He says, "Civilized humankind has been getting it wrong…Cease to eat anything defiled by violence; make your table the high altar of your daily religion; serve nothing that is produced by harming the land and its life or by any kind of cruelty; then the rest follows."

I love eating locally and organically, as I know it helps the earth, but the idea of only eating animals I cherish is a bit much for me. I just can't pull that one off. I know how most animals live and die in this country and it is shameful to say the least. I avoid eating four-leggeds, so I guess the parents on the farm would say I could go ahead and name the creatures.

But what is this obsession with naming everything really about? My friends are often aghast that I can't name all the perennials in my garden. "You must learn the names," they say emphatically as if it is a given. Why? Why must I learn the names? Native people would say the name is the least important thing to learn about something. You have to learn its essence. Observe its ways of being. Feel its particular uniqueness. Observe its preferences. Even talk to it and listen for its language. See if it has a message for you. And then later, if you have time, you can learn its name. But don't assume you know something just because you have its name memorized.

As I write this, my one-eyed friend arrives. We are sitting in the sun on the porch steps. I stop to feed her seed from my hand and now she is full. Now that she's got the goods, will she run off? No, it seems she is lingering by my side, licking her paw. We are content, the two of us. We are basking in the sun – together!

Now I must decide. Should I give her a name? I hate all those cheesy names that humans give animals. My friend is strong and brave. She needs a dignified name if at all – like Antoinette. But that is such a human frame of reference. She needs a name that is all about chipmunks, in their own style, like Schwizzle or Whabitz, or Durlong. I think I like Durlong as she has long endured her affliction. I turn to her and ask if she has a name. We make prolonged eye contact and stare inquisitively. Anyway, I will wait and see if her name is unveiled. She is gone now, but next time she might surprise me. She may be a he!

HUMMER VIGNETTES

A hummer is right on the clothesline as I hang up our clothes. Does it see me? It is so near I could reach out and touch it. But I don't. Instead I freeze, doing my best to look non-threatening. It glances at me. I try to avoid staring, but I can't. It is too precious. I must observe every detail. Its beak is slightly open, almost as if smacking its lips. It cocks its head as it observes me. What is it doing, trying to turn me inside out with delight? I keep thinking our time is up and it will surely flee. But for some unknown reason, it lingers as if allowing me to become entirely enchanted. And then it lifts its wings to fly away, but it doesn't. It simply turns and faces the other direction. Now I have a full view of its glistening emerald feathers. I have to contain my urge to touch such delicacy.

I decide to move a bit, testing the limits of this comfort between us. As I move slowly it remains. I accidentally make some noise and it flees. Still I am stunned. It has cast a spell over me and I too am "humming" with joy.

A hummer is chasing the others, darting at them with its lethal beak extended. I have just put out fresh food in the feeder. It has three holes and plenty of juice. There are three hummers fighting for dominance over the feeder. There are three holes and three hummers! They are fighting as if there were one hole and a scarcity of juice. Now they are all chasing in a big circle it seems. Each one is being pursued by another. Rarely does one succeed at getting a drink. They are too busy having their senseless, unnecessary feud. I am watching a long time, hoping to see a resolution or a peaceful settlement. Even a compromise would do. But all I see is more fighting. Before too long one of them will get weary and submit. How sad.

A hummer is right near my shoulder as I water the garden. It actually startles me. It flies toward the jet of water. I move as little as possible so that the spray of water remains stationary. It flies under the water and then back up to a nearby branch. Then it flies up to the water – seemingly drinking. Then it backs off again. Next it bravely circles the water – over, under, up, down, in, out, and through. It is clearly enjoying this. Next it just hovers under the water where the soft sprinkles are falling. I wonder when it will dart away. It doesn't. It remains transfixed by this waterspout. The garden is getting well drenched as this goes on and on. This hummer is playing! There is no other possible explanation. It has already bathed and drunk from the water. It is lingering just to play. It is soaring into the spray from every angle and then encircles the jet over and over. This feels strangely familiar, like holding the sprinkler for my children when they were very young.

FREDDIE

Freddie has been living in our pond for many years now. Green frogs have a life span of only five to eight years. So each spring when Freddie reappears at his perching spot, I am relieved and amazed he has survived another Michigan winter. I am embarrassed to say that I named Freddie years ago and never really bothered to confirm that it was in fact a male frog. So, becoming convinced that I needed to do a better job of getting to know my neighbors, I began to do research. I learned that the circle behind Freddie's eye, his eardrum, was the key to determining his gender. If the circle is larger than the eye circle, then the green frog is a male. If it is equal in size or smaller, it is a female. I also learned that the female green frog has a white chest and the male has a yellow chest. So I learned that Freddie is in fact a female! No, I didn't rename her. She is "Freddie the female frog!"

But Freddie has become more unpredictable in her old age. She has begun to take long vacations and can disappear for a week or more at a time only to return again and again. For all I know, she goes no farther than the bushes that obscure her view. But during these times I am known to check the pond often throughout the day, looking for my lost frog friend who is nowhere in view.

The first time Freddie was gone for a long vacation, I became increasingly convinced she had become snake food or raccoon dinner. I began telling my friends, "Freddie is gone – I think this

is the end." By the end of the second week, others were beginning to believe my conclusion as well, except for my friend Susan. She is an Episcopal priest and is obviously well trained in offering pastoral presence to those grieving lost frog friends. "I will pray that Freddie returns," she assured me. Was she joking or did I detect that she, too, had been converted into a frog lover? All I know is that it seemed right that she was visiting the day that Freddie returned. She hollered at me with urgency in her voice, "Hurry, come quickly, Freddie is back!"

I figured she wasn't too good at discerning one frog from another and that it was most likely a new frog, but I ran to her side and began to inspect. Looking carefully, with hope and joy rising within, I began to beam. "I think you're right, Susan, that sure looks like Freddie." If I had any doubts, what transpired next left me certain that it was in fact the return of Freddie. At the distant side of the pond, she was perched on her favorite little hill of sedum. I was directly across the pond, close to the edge beaming at Freddie with delight. "Freddie, where have you been? I'm so glad you are back." Could she feel the warmth I was exuding toward her? Was she glad to see me too? All I know is that Freddie chose that precise moment to jump in the water, swim directly across the pond, crawl out of the water and climb right up to my fingers that were extended toward her. Then we did what we often do. I tickled her belly with a moistened finger as we lingered awhile - together again!

DEER-MENTORS

You ask my ancestry?
German, maybe Irish,
I don't know, but
This I do know.
I am part deer!
What part?
The part that must
Take refuge in the
Gentle forest of white pines,
Making my day-bed in
Soft carpet of fallen needles,
Smelling moist rich soil
As I curl up as close
As I can to this
Earth we call Mother.
She welcomes me so
strongly,

As if pulling me into
My forgotten Self,
The one that
Resides at the
Juncture of skin and soil.
There I sit with my
Back against the shelter
Of Tree Trunk,
Hoping to blend into the
Beauty that surrounds,
Hoping to become
Part of it All,
Trying to be as
Quiet within
As nearby deer-mentors,
Masters of
Stillness.

RESOURCES

If you are interested in learning more about the content of bird communication systems, I highly recommend the works of Jon Young, an expert on nature awareness. His knowledge is probably rivaled only by the Bushmen of the Kalahari. I am an avid fan of his CD series entitled *Advanced Bird Language*. Both the CD and his new book, *What the Robin Knows*, published by Houghton Mifflin Harcourt, 2012, can be purchased on his website at www.jonyoung.org.

To learn more about the extent to which humans can communicate with wild animals, I highly recommend the book, *Adventures in Kinship With All Life*, written by J. Allen Boone and published by Tree of Life Books, 1990. His sensitivity to and rapport with wild creatures is remarkable.

Page 45 David Abram speaks of our "more-than-human" friends in his book, *The Spell of the Sensuous*, published by Vintage Books, 1996. He passionately writes about interspecies communication and about our place in the wider natural community. Abram is an exceptionally sensitive writer and gifted speaker.

Page 45 Derrick Jensen is a prolific and gifted writer. I am especially grateful for his book, *A Language Older Than Words*, published by Context Books, 2000. He deeply understands the language and the value of all creatures.

Page 64 To learn more about the Hopi understanding of the "Four Worlds," the "Song of Creation," or the "Original Instructions," I strongly recommend the book, *Meditations With the Hopi*, by Robert Boissiere and published by Bear and Co., 1986.

Page 70 To read more about a great man who was dedicated to interspecies community, read *Sanctuary For All Life* written by Jim Corbett and published by Howling Dog Press, 2005. His perspective on eating animals is unique.

Purchase additional copies online at
www.allearthtiles.com

27458974R00047